The Wonder of
DOLPHINS

To Anne, Jennifer, Andy, Nick, Jaclyn, Katie, and Rachel – and all kids
who love dolphins.   — Patricia Corrigan

**For a free color catalog describing Gareth Stevens' list of high-quality books and
multimedia programs, call 1-800-542-2595 (USA) or 1-800-461-9120 (Canada).
Gareth Stevens Publishing's Fax: (414) 225-0377.
See our catalog, too, on the World Wide Web: http://gsinc.com**

Library of Congress Cataloging-in-Publication Data

Ritchie, Rita.
    The wonder of dolphins / by Rita Ritchie and Patricia Corrigan ;
  photographs by Flip Nicklin ; illustrations by John F. McGee.
       p. cm. — (Animal wonders)
    "Based on . . . Dolphin magic for kids . . . by Patricia Corrigan"—
T.p. verso.
    Includes index.
    Summary: Text and photographs introduce some of the thirty-nine different kinds of dolphins.
    ISBN 0-8368-1559-9 (lib. bdg.)
    1. Dolphins—Juvenile literature. [1. Dolphins.] I. Corrigan, Patricia, 1948- . II. Nicklin, Flip, ill.
III. McGee, John F., ill. IV. Corrigan, Patricia, 1948- Dolphins. V. Title. VI. Series.
QL737.C432R58   1996
599.5'3--dc20   96-5005

First published in North America in 1996 by
Gareth Stevens Publishing
1555 North RiverCenter Drive, Suite 201
Milwaukee, WI 53212 USA

This edition is based on the book *Dolphin Magic for Kids* © 1995 by Patricia Corrigan, first
published in the United States in 1995 by NorthWord Press, Inc., Minocqua, Wisconsin, and
published in a library edition by Gareth Stevens, Inc., in 1995. All photographs © 1995 by
Flip Nicklin/Minden Pictures except pp. 44-45, © Sam Abell/National Geographic Society, with
illustrations by John F. McGee. Additional end matter © 1996 by Gareth Stevens, Inc.

Printed in the United States of America

1 2 3 4 5 6 7 8 9 99 98 97 96

The Wonder of
DOLPHINS

by Rita Ritchie and Patricia Corrigan
Photographs by Flip Nicklin
Illustrations by John F. McGee

Gareth Stevens Publishing
MILWAUKEE

People like to read about
dolphins, watch them in
zoos and water parks, and
see them in movies and
on television.

Dolphins are mammals that
have lived for fifty million
years. They give birth to
live young that they nurse.
Dolphins live in water, but
they must come up for air.

With its head above water, a dolphin blows out old air and breathes in fresh air. It then closes its blowhole and dives under the water.

Bottlenose dolphin

There are thirty-nine different kinds of dolphins. Some have the word *whale* as part of their name, but they are really dolphins.

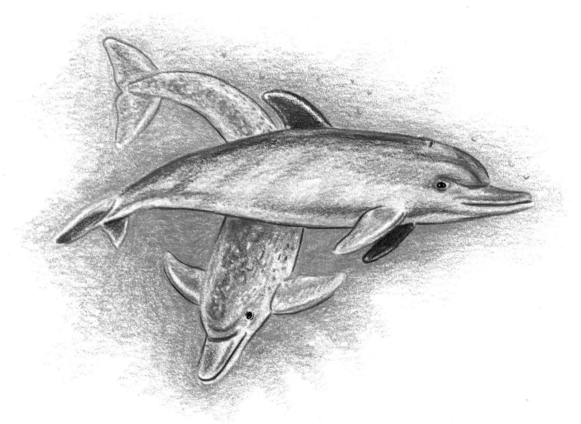

The beluga is a creamy white dolphin that lives in the Arctic. Belugas make a chirping sound and are called "the canaries of the sea."

Beluga

Striped dolphins and spotted dolphins live in all the oceans. Black dolphins live off the coast of Chile.

Spotted dolphin

A dolphin has a big flipper on each side of its body. The tail of a dolphin is called a fluke. A dolphin can swim at speeds of 25 miles (40 kilometers) an hour.

Dolphins have teeth. In the male narwhal dolphin, one tooth grows into a tusk almost 10 feet (3 meters) long. It can weigh up to 20 pounds (9 kilograms).

Narwhal dolphins

Hector's dolphin is small. It is 5 feet (1.5 m) long and weighs 125 pounds (57 kg). But the smallest dolphin is the vaquita at 4 feet (1.2 m) long and 100 pounds (45 kg).

Hector's dolphin

The biggest
dolphin is the
killer whale, or
orca. Its skin is
black and white.
It has a tall,
straight fin
on its back.

Orca

Orcas grow to 30 feet (9 m) long and can weigh 10 tons (9 metric tons). They eat 400 pounds (180 kg) of food a day.

Dolphins make click and whistle sounds. The sounds bounce off objects, and a dolphin's jaw picks up the echoes. A dolphin's brain can identify the objects as well as their size and location.

This system is called echolocation.
It helps the dolphin find food and
navigate, or figure out where it
is and where it is going.

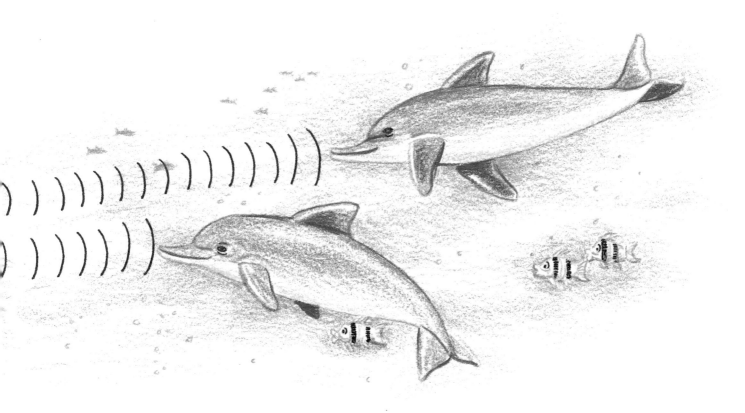

Fishermen tell stories about how dolphins often come near their boats at sea.

Bottlenose dolphins sometimes swim near boats. They like to ride the wake, or waves, that boats make.

Dolphins jump and dive as if they are playing.

Dolphins are smart. Their brains are very large – the same size as the brains of gorillas. Dolphins even communicate with each other. They "talk" with a series of clicks and whistles.

Some dolphins live in rivers in China, India, and South America. Certain dolphins that live along sea coasts also swim up rivers.

Boutu dolphin

The boutu dolphin lives in the Amazon River in South America. It is born dark gray, but later turns pink. There is a legend that says pink dolphins come out of the river at night and turn into people with red hair. Then they put on hats to hide their blowholes and go dancing!

Legend has it that dolphins have saved shipwrecked sailors.

Dolphins face dangers, such as pollution, hunting, and getting trapped in fishing nets. Dolphins can become stranded on shore.

We must all help dolphins survive. Maybe one day you'll see Funghie, a bottlenose dolphin. Funghie greets fishing boats off the coast of Ireland.

Funghie the dolphin

A famous author, Herman Melville, said that dolphins "keep tossing themselves to heaven like caps in a Fourth-of-July crowd."

Glossary

blowhole – a "nostril" on top of the head of a dolphin, whale, or porpoise

echolocation – a way an animal locates objects by using sound waves that echo, or bounce back, to the animal

flipper – a wide, flat limb on an animal that is used for swimming

fluke – the tail of a dolphin

mammal – an animal with hair or fur that feeds its young with mother's milk

navigate – to find the course or way to travel

nurse – to feed the young with mother's milk

stranded – when a dolphin or other animal is beached or stuck on land

tusk – a long, pointed tooth that projects outside the closed mouth of an animal

wake – the track or path of waves left in the water by a moving boat or other object

Index